Kathy Casey Cooks

favorites

Cover and interior design:
Alicia Nammacher
Cover and interior photographs:
E. Jane Armstrong
Cover portrait and studio photo:
Saundra Velencia
Food styling: Kathy Casey,
Kim Holderman, Diana Isaiou,
Jane Morimoto, Charlotte Rudge,
Patty Wittmann
Proofreading and indexing:
Miriam Bulmer
Special thanks to: Renée Hinrichs

Library of Congress Cataloging
in Publication Data
Casey, Kathy.
Kathy Casey Cooks Favorites /
by Kathy Casey; photography
by E. Jane Armstrong

ISBN-13: 978-0-9708751-0-5
ISBN-10: 0-9708751-0-X
1. Cookery. I. Title.

Published by Kathy Casey Food
Studios / Kathy Casey Inc.
5130 Ballard Avenue Northwest
Seattle, Washington 98107
206.784.7840
info@kathycasey.com
http://www.kathycasey.com

I have compiled this book as the first of a series for fellow cooks and foodies. As with all aspects of life, cooking should be fun and an enjoyable art—not a daunting task. So whether you are a weekend cook, a true cookbook-combing gourmet or a spur-of-the-moment concoctor of great ingredients, I hope that these recipes will either give you delicious pleasure or inspire your own culinary adventure. Cook up some fun! —Kathy Casey

———————

To John and all our delicious times together.

———————

contents

6 sips & apps
18 starters
30 comfort
44 sides
50 mains
62 conclusions
79 index

1

Love Potion No.10
Makes 1 cocktail

2 oz. Tanqueray Ten gin
2 oz. Love Potion Mix (recipe follows)
Garnish: 1 frozen whole cranberry

Fill shaker with ice; add Ten and Love Potion Mix. Shake until
mixture is very cold. Strain drink into large martini glass. Float whole
cranberry on top of drink.

Love Potion Mix — *makes enough for 8 cocktails*
1/2 cup apricot nectar   1/2 cup simple syrup
1/4 cup fresh lemon juice   2 Tbsp. cranberry juice
6 Tbsp. fresh lime juice   1/4 cup fresh tangerine juice

Zoë Cocktail
Makes 1 cocktail

Created as a signature cocktail for my friends Scott and
Heather Staples' Restaurant Zoë

1/4 oz. blue curaçao   2 big sprigs of mint
2 oz. Bacardi limon rum   Garnish: mint leaf
2 oz. Lime Sour (recipe follows)

Fill shaker with ice, add curaçao, rum, lime sour and mint sprigs.
Shake until very cold. Strain drink into large martini glass.
Float mint leaf on top of drink.

Lime Sour — *makes 2 cups*
1 cup fresh lime juice
1 cup simple syrup

Combine and keep refrigerated.

To make your own simple syrup: Combine equal parts of
sugar and water, and boil for 3 minutes.

Roasted Tiny Red Potatoes with Caviar & Shallot Sour Cream or Gorgonzola Bacon & Walnuts

Each topping recipe makes enough for 12 potatoes.
If serving both toppings, double the potato recipe.

12 very small red potatoes, washed
  (approx. 1 to 1 1/4 lb.)
1 Tbsp. olive oil

1/2 tsp. salt
1/4 tsp. black pepper

Preheat oven to 400° F.

In a medium bowl toss together potatoes, olive oil, salt and pepper. Spread potatoes out on a baking sheet and place in preheated oven. Bake for 25 minutes or until tender. Keep warm. Right before serving, cut potatoes in half, cutting a little piece from bottoms if they don't stand up. Top potatoes as described in topping recipes.

1/2 cup sour cream (or substitute
nonfat sour cream)
3 Tbsp. thinly sliced fresh chives

1 Tbsp. very finely minced shallot
2 oz. high-quality caviar

Shallot Sour Cream Topping & Caviar
In a small bowl combine the sour cream, 2 Tbsp. of the chives and the shallots. Cover and refrigerate until needed. Top each potato piece with a tsp. of sour cream topping and a dollop of caviar. Sprinkle with remaining chives.

6 slices bacon
1/4 cup walnuts,
  toasted and chopped
1/2 cup sour cream
1/4 cup Gorgonzola cheese, crumbled

2 Tbsp. thinly sliced fresh chives
1/4 tsp. salt
1/8 tsp. black pepper
1/8 tsp. Tabasco Sauce

Gorgonzola Bacon & Walnut Topping
In a medium skillet over medium-high heat, cook bacon until crispy, approximately 4 to 5 minutes. Drain bacon, then chop. In a small bowl combine walnuts and bacon with sour cream. Mix in Gorgonzola, one Tbsp. of the chives (reserve remaining chives for garnish), salt, pepper and Tabasco. Top each potato piece with a tsp. of Gorgonzola topping. Sprinkle with remaining chives. Serve warm.

Gin Infused Prawns with Martini Aïoli
Makes about 24 to 30 prawns and 1 1/2 cups of aïoli

Martini Aïoli
2 Tbsp. fresh lemon juice
2 raw egg yolks*
1 tsp. minced garlic
1/2 tsp. juniper berries,
  crushed and finely chopped
1 1/2 tsp. minced lemon zest
1/2 tsp. salt
1/8 tsp. black pepper
3/4 tsp. Dijon mustard
1/16 tsp. cayenne pepper
1/2 cup light/fruity olive oil
1/2 cup salad oil
1 1/2 tsp. gin

1/3 cup minced stuffed
  green olives, drained
3 Tbsp. minced cocktail onions
1 Tbsp. finely chopped
  Italian parsley

Prawns
1/2 cup dry white vermouth
1/4 cup gin
1 tsp. juniper berries, crushed
1/8 tsp. black pepper
1/8 tsp. salt
1 1/2 lb. large prawns
  in the shell, peeled and deveined

To make the aïoli: In food processor combine lemon juice, egg yolks, garlic, juniper berries, zest, salt, pepper, mustard and cayenne, and process to thoroughly combine. With processor running, gradually drizzle in oils, emulsifying aïoli. The consistency should be thick and smooth, like mayonnaise. Add remaining ingredients and pulse.

To cook the prawns: Place the vermouth, gin, juniper berries, pepper and salt in a medium-large pot with a tight-fitting lid. Place over high heat and bring to a quick boil. Add the prawns and stir them in. Cover and steam for 1 minute. Remove the lid and stir the prawns. Place the lid back on and cook until prawns are a little more than 3/4 cooked, about 1/2 to 1 minute more. Remove pan from heat and let prawns cool in cooking mixture to finish cooking, stirring occasionally. Cool prawns in liquid in the refrigerator until well chilled before serving.

Serving suggestions: Place a little pouf of gourmet greens in the bottom of a small martini glass. Place a dollop of Martini Aïoli in the center and hang a few prawns off the rim of the glass. Or, if you have a great collection of shot glasses, place a prawn in a shot glass and dollop with a little of the aïoli.

* Note: Raw eggs are not recommended for pregnant women, children, the elderly or anyone with immune deficiencies.

Ribbons of Roasted Peppers &
Herb Goat Cheese on Crostini
Makes about 20 pieces; double the recipe for a large crowd!

2 large red bell peppers
2 Tbsp. extra virgin olive oil
2 Tbsp. balsamic vinegar
1/2 tsp. salt

3/4 cup chèvre goat cheese
2 Tbsp. minced, mixed fresh herbs,
  such as basil, thyme, oregano, marjoram
20 crostini (recipe follows)

Roast peppers over a hot grill or coals, over a gas flame, under a broiler, or in a 500° F oven, turning often until skin is totally blistered and charred black. Immediately place in a bowl and cover with plastic wrap to steam skins loose. Let cool until peppers can be handled, about 15 to 20 minutes. Slip skin off, seed and slice peppers into thin strips. Place in a bowl and add the olive oil, vinegar and salt. Toss.

In a small bowl mix together the goat cheese and the fresh herbs. Top the crostini with the peppers and a dollop of the goat cheese. Sprinkle with a little fresh herbs or kalamata olives if desired for garnish.

Crostini
Makes about 40 pieces

1 long, skinny French or Italian rustic baguette
Olive oil as needed
Kosher salt

Preheat oven to 400° F.

Slice bread into 1/8-inch to 1/4-inch slices and very lightly brush with olive oil. If doing a large batch, try putting olive oil in a new, clean spray bottle and lightly misting the tops. Place bread in a single layer on baking sheets and toast in oven until just crispy.

Flat Bread Crisps with
Smoked Salmon & Chive Sour Cream
Makes 18 pieces

I love this served with chilled glasses of bubbly!

1/3 cup sour cream (or substitute nonfat sour cream)
2 Tbsp. thinly sliced fresh chives
1 Tbsp. very finely minced red onion
1/3 cup diced and seeded cucumber, very small
1 Tbsp. seasoned rice wine vinegar
6 thin slices cold-smoked salmon
Flat bread, enough to break into about
  18 appetizer-size pieces, or crostini
Extra fresh chives for garnish
Lemon zest for garnish

To make the chive sour cream: In a small bowl combine the
sour cream, 2 Tbsp. of chives and red onion. Cover and
refrigerate until needed.

To serve: Mix cucumber with seasoned rice wine vinegar.
Let marinate at least 10 minutes.

Cut each piece of smoked salmon into 3 pieces. Top each flat-
bread piece with a dollop (about 1 tsp.) of the sour cream and
then a tsp. of the cucumbers. (Be sure to drain any excess juice
off cucumbers before using.) Top with a piece of smoked salmon.
You can also lay the salmon out flat on the flat bread or crostini
and then dollop with the sour cream and cucumbers.

Garnish with fresh chives and lemon zest if desired.

starters

2

Merlot "Double Red Wine" Vinaigrette with Simple Seasonal Greens

Makes 1 1/2 cups vinaigrette

This dressing is intense, flavorful and super with robust greens such as arugula, Belgian endive and radicchio. I also love to serve the greens with slices of orange and red onion for the play of flavors.

Mixed seasonal greens, as desired
Sliced red onions (optional)
Sliced oranges (optional)

Vinaigrette
1/2 cup Merlot red wine
1/2 cup red wine vinegar
1 1/2 tsp. Dijon mustard
1/2 tsp. finely minced garlic
1 Tbsp. finely minced shallots
1/2 tsp. salt
1/4 tsp. black pepper
1 cup extra virgin olive oil
1/2 tsp. minced fresh rosemary

In a small noncorrosive saucepan, combine the wine and wine vinegar, place over high heat and bring to a boil. Continue boiling until liquid is reduced (by half) to 1/2 cup. Remove from heat and cool to room temperature.

Place the cooled red wine reduction in a medium bowl. Add the mustard, garlic, shallots, salt and pepper. Whisk together, then slowly drizzle in the olive oil while whisking continuously. Then stir in the rosemary. Mixture should be nicely emulsified. Refrigerate until needed, whisking well again before serving.

To serve: In a large bowl place about 1 Tbsp. vinaigrette for every super-packed, heaping cup of greens. This dressing is big flavored, so not much is needed per serving. With clean hands, toss well, being sure to coat each leaf with dressing. Add more dressing or greens to taste.

Orange, Avocado & Red Onion "Jumble" with Poppyseed Vinaigrette
Makes 4 cups, about 6 servings

3 large oranges
1 cup thinly sliced red onion
2 ripe but firm avocados

Poppyseed Vinaigrette
3 Tbsp. white wine vinegar

1 tsp. finely minced fresh ginger
2 Tbsp. Dijon mustard
3 Tbsp. honey
1/4 cup salad oil or light olive oil
2 tsp. poppy seeds
2 Tbsp. chopped Italian parsley

Make the vinaigrette first: Combine all ingredients in a bowl and whisk together until smooth. Chill until ready to serve salad.

Cut ends off oranges and then cut skin off the sides of oranges, carefully removing all the white pith. Cut oranges in half lengthwise, seed and then cut into 1/4-inch slices. Place in a large bowl with onion. Cut avocados in quarters, peel and then slice into salad. Toss with dressing and serve.

Golden Beet Salad with Arugula & Balsamic Vinaigrette
Makes 4 salads

4 medium-size golden beets,
    about the size of large lemons
    (substitute red beets if desired)
2 Tbsp. orange juice
1 Tbsp. balsamic vinegar
1/2 tsp. sugar

1 Tbsp. olive oil
1/4 tsp. salt
6 cups baby or regular
    arugula, washed
    and spun dry
Freshly ground black pepper

Peel beets and cut into 1/2-inch wedges; you should have about 2 cups. Steam beets until totally tender. Refrigerate until chilled.

In a large bowl whisk together the orange juice, balsamic vinegar, sugar, olive oil and salt. Toss the beets with the dressing and let stand, refrigerated, for about 30 minutes.

Remove the beets from the dressing and divide them among 4 plates, reserving the dressing. Add the arugula to the remaining dressing in the bowl and toss well. Divide among the 4 plates. Sprinkle with freshly ground pepper if desired. Serve at once.

Spinach Salad with Apples & Warm Bacon Vinaigrette

Serves 4 to 6 as a starter salad

1 bunch fresh spinach, stemmed,
  washed well and dried (about 4 packed cups)
1 Fuji apple, cored and thinly sliced

Warm Bacon Vinaigrette
1/4 cup finely diced raw bacon
1/4 cup finely diced red onion
1/4 cup thinly sliced shiitake mushrooms,
  stemmed (optional)
1 tsp. minced garlic
2 tsp. Dijon mustard
1/4 cup white vinegar
2 Tbsp. sugar
1/8 tsp. crushed red chile flakes
1/2 tsp. black pepper
1/4 tsp. salt
2 Tbsp. extra virgin olive oil

Place spinach and apple slices in a large bowl
and refrigerate until ready to dress.

In a small nonstick pan cook the bacon over medium-high
heat until half done, about 2 to 3 minutes. Add onion,
mushrooms and garlic, and cook until onion is barely
tender, about 1 minute.

In a small bowl whisk together remaining dressing
ingredients and then stir into pan. Immediately remove
from heat and pour over spinach and apples. Toss until
salad is well coated with dressing. Serve immediately.

Vine-Ripe Tomato & Fresh Mozzarella "Caprese" Tower with Quick Basil Aïoli

Serves 4

4 medium, vine-ripe tomatoes
4 medium to large fresh
    mozzarella balls (the kind
    that are packed in water),
    drained well

1 bunch arugula, washed
    and dried (about 2 cups)
Kosher salt
4 basil sprigs
Freshly ground pepper

Quick Basil Aïoli

1 tsp. finely minced fresh garlic
1 Tbsp. fresh lemon juice
1/4 cup extra virgin olive oil
2 Tbsp. chopped fresh basil

3 Tbsp. high-quality
    mayonnaise, such
    as Best Foods

<u>Make the aïoli first</u>: In a blender process the garlic, lemon juice, olive oil and basil together until smooth. Place mixture into a small bowl and whisk in the mayonnaise until emulsified. Chill until needed. Can be made up to 2 days in advance.

<u>To assemble the salad</u>: With a paring knife cut the top stem out of each tomato and a thin slice off the bottom so the tomatoes will stand up. Then slice each tomato into 4 even, horizontal slices. Set aside.

Cut each mozzarella ball into 3 to 6 slices. (If ball is on the smaller side, you will need to put two pieces/slices on a couple of layers.)

On 4 large salad or dinner plates divide the arugula evenly into little nests, about 5 inches across, in the center of each plate, being sure to leave some nice "white space" on the plate. Reassemble each sliced tomato in the center of the greens, sprinkling each layer of tomato with a little kosher salt and dabbing with a scant tsp. of the aïoli, then inserting a slice of cheese. Finish with the top slice of tomato. Drizzle 1 Tbsp. of the extra aïoli on greens and plate in an artistic manner. Insert fresh basil sprigs in the top of each tomato where the stem was cut out. Serve immediately, with a steak knife with each salad. Grind a little fresh black pepper on the salads at the table, if desired.

Ribollita Soup with Extra Virgin Olive Oil
Makes 6 to 8 servings

A Tuscan favorite, this hearty soup thickened with stale bread is traditionally "twice boiled"—cooked, then reheated the next day. The flavorful olive oil, which is always drizzled on top right before eating, acts like a seasoning, giving this soup a special little kick.

3 Tbsp. chopped bacon
1 Tbsp. olive oil
3/4 cup diced onion
1 cup diced red potatoes
1/8 tsp. crushed red chile flakes
2 cloves garlic, minced
3/4 cup diced carrot
3/4 cup diced celery
3/4 tsp. dry thyme leaves
2 cups packed, torn, dark green kale

4 cups rich chicken broth
1 cup chopped fresh tomatoes
  with juice
1 can (15 oz.) cannellini
  beans with liquid
2 cups, packed, rustic Italian
  bread, preferably stale, torn
  into bite-size pieces
Salt and pepper to taste
Extra virgin olive oil for drizzling

Heat a large soup kettle or Dutch oven over medium-high heat. Add bacon and olive oil and cook until 3/4 done. Add onion and potatoes, and cook, stirring often, about 2 to 3 minutes. Add the chile flakes, garlic, carrots and celery. Cook, stirring, about 1 to 2 more minutes. Add the thyme, kale, chicken broth and tomatoes. Bring to a simmer and cook slowly for about 12 minutes.

Add the beans and bean liquid and bread. Stir in and cook about 2 more minutes, or until thickened with the bread. Season with salt and pepper to taste.

To serve: Ladle into bowls and drizzle liberally with olive oil.

If the soup is made a day ahead, it will be thicker the next day, almost stew-like, but this is the traditional way. If it is too thick for your liking, thin with a little chicken stock when reheating.

comfort

3

"Denver" Breakfast Bake for a Crowd
Serves 6 to 8

2 Tbsp. butter or olive oil
3/4 cup diced onion
1 1/2 cups julienne (matchstick-cut),
    mixed red and green bell peppers
1 Tbsp. minced fresh garlic
8 eggs
3 cups half-and-half
1 tsp. salt
1/4 tsp. black pepper
8 cups 1-inch-diced hearty French bread
1 1/2 cups julienne (matchstick-cut) ham
2 cups (8 oz.) coarsely grated
    cheddar cheese
3 Tbsp. sliced green onion
1/2 cup grated Parmesan cheese

In a large sauté pan heat the butter or olive oil over medium-high
heat. Add the onion and peppers, and sauté until 3/4 cooked, about
4 minutes. Add the garlic and cook for 30 seconds more. Remove
from heat and set aside.

In a large bowl whisk together the eggs, half-and-half, salt and
pepper until well combined. Add the bread, ham, cooled vegetables,
cheddar cheese, green onion and half of the Parmesan cheese. Place
in an 11-by-13-inch baking pan. Sprinkle the remaining Parmesan
over the top and let sit, refrigerated, at least 1 hour or preferably
overnight, so that the bread soaks up the egg mixture.

When ready to serve, bake in a preheated 350° F oven for
approximately 45 to 50 minutes, or until puffy and golden and
a knife inserted in the center comes out clean.

Cornmeal Griddle Cakes
Makes about 16 griddle cakes

1 cup water	1 1/2 tsp. baking powder
1 1/4 cups milk	1/2 tsp. salt
1 Tbsp. sugar	4 Tbsp. melted butter
1/2 cup yellow cornmeal	2 eggs, slightly beaten
1 cup flour	3/4 cup milk

In a heavy-bottomed, medium saucepan bring water, 1 1/4 cups milk and sugar just to a simmer. Slowly sprinkle in cornmeal, whisking continuously so no lumps form. Slowly simmer, stirring frequently and adjusting heat, until cornmeal is tender, about 4 minutes. Pour into a large bowl to cool to room temperature, stirring occasionally to prevent a skin from forming.

Meanwhile, sift together flour, baking powder and salt in a small bowl. Set aside.

When cornmeal mixture has cooled, stir in melted butter and eggs, mixing until smooth. Stir in flour mixture and remaining milk. Batter should be fairly smooth.

Heat griddle over about medium heat. If needed, drizzle with about 1 tsp. oil, then wipe with a triple-folded paper towel to just lightly oil the surface.

For each cake, ladle 1/4 cup batter onto heated griddle. Turn pancakes when they are slightly puffy (note: this type has very few bubbles compared to regular-style pancakes) and golden brown, and brown on other side.

Brown Sugar & Pepper Glazed Bacon
Serves 6 to 8

1 lb. thick-sliced bacon	2 tsp. balsamic or cider vinegar
1 Tbsp. Dijon mustard	3/4 tsp. coarsely ground
3 Tbsp. brown sugar	black pepper

Preheat oven to 350° F. Lay out the bacon on a sided baking sheet. Bake in oven until about 3/4 done. Drain well and dab with paper towels.

Meanwhile, in a very small saucepan, heat remaining ingredients until smooth. Using a pastry brush, brush bacon with some of the glaze.

Increase oven to 425° F. Bake bacon for about 5 to 7 minutes, or until crispy and glazy.

comfort

The Best Blue Cheese-Stuffed Burgers on Garlic Buns with Vine-Ripe Tomatoes & Horseradish Spread

Makes 6 half-pound burgers

Burger
3 lb. lean ground beef
1 tsp. salt
1/4 tsp. pepper
1 Tbsp. soy sauce
4 tsp. Worcestershire sauce
1 Tbsp. chopped garlic
4 oz. blue cheese

Horseradish Spread
1/2 cup high-quality mayonnaise
1 Tbsp. creamed horseradish
2 tsp. grainy mustard

6 homemade Garlic Burger Buns (recipe follows)
    or 6 high quality hamburger buns spread with garlic butter
Thick-sliced, vine-ripened tomatoes
Fresh arugula or lettuce

Horseradish Spread: Mix together spread ingredients and set aside. Mix meat, salt, pepper, soy sauce, Worcestershire sauce and garlic until thoroughly combined. Shape beef into 6 equal balls.

Divide cheese into 6 pieces/balls and press into the center of the meat. Press out into 5-inch patties, being sure that the meat is surrounding the cheese in the middle.

To grill and serve: Heat charcoal or gas grill until very hot. Set patties apart on grill, turning when first side is browned. Cook to desired doneness, about 4 minutes per side depending on your heat.

Split buns and toast lightly. Place burgers on buns and serve with tomato slices, arugula or lettuce leaves, and a dollop of Horseradish Spread, as desired.

Garlic Burger Buns
Makes 6 buns

1/2 cup milk
1 Tbsp. olive oil
2 Tbsp. sugar
1/3 cup warm water (90° F to 110° F)
1 package dry yeast (2 1/4 tsp.)
2 eggs
3 cups all-purpose flour
3/4 tsp. salt
1 Tbsp. finely minced garlic
Kosher salt for sprinkling

In a small bowl stir together the milk, olive oil, sugar, warm water
and yeast. Stir to dissolve yeast and let sit about 10 minutes,
then pour into a large mixer bowl.

Whisk the eggs in a small bowl and add all but 1 Tbsp. to the liquid
ingredients, reserving the extra for brushing the bun tops. Mix in flour,
salt and garlic with paddle attachment until incorporated and then
change to a dough hook. Mix with dough hook on medium speed for
about 3 to 4 minutes, as needed, to make a smooth, moist dough.
Knead until smooth. Place in a large greased bowl, cover with a towel
and let rise in a warm place until doubled, about 1 1/2 hours.

Punch down and divide dough into 6 pieces. Roll into balls and let
rest 10 minutes covered with a towel. With a well-floured rolling pin,
roll balls into 4-inch rounds. Place on a greased baking sheet.
Cover lightly with a towel and let rise until almost doubled.

Meanwhile, preheat oven to 350° F

In a small bowl, whisk remaining egg together with 1/2 Tbsp. water.
Brush the tops of the buns lightly with egg wash, sprinkle lightly with
coarse kosher salt and place in oven.

Bake about 15 to 20 minutes, or until golden brown. Cool buns on a rack.

comfort

4 Cheese "Mac" with Herb Bread Crumbs

Generously serves 6 to 8

4 Tbsp. butter or margarine
1 Tbsp. minced garlic
4 1/2 Tbsp. flour
4 cups whole milk or half-and-half
1 1/2 tsp. salt
1/4 tsp. black pepper
1 cup sour cream
1/4 cup grated high-quality
   Parmesan cheese
1 lb. dry cavatappi pasta
2 cups (1/2 lb.) grated
   four-cheese blend

2 cups (1/2 lb.) grated
   cheddar cheese
1/2 cup milk

Herb Bread Crumbs
3 cups, packed, 1-inch
   French bread chunks
4 Tbsp. butter
Pinch of salt and pepper
2 Tbsp. chopped fresh parsley
1/2 tsp. dry basil leaves
1/2 tsp. dry thyme leaves

Preheat oven to 375° F.

To make bread crumbs: Place bread crumb ingredients in food processor, and pulse until the bread becomes fine crumbs and is well mixed. Set aside.

In a large heavy-bottomed saucepan melt the butter over medium heat. Add the garlic and stir for about 20 seconds; do not let garlic brown. Stir in the flour and cook for about 1 minute, stirring constantly. While stirring vigorously with a whisk, add the milk. Whisk well. Bring to a simmer and whisk occasionally until sauce is thickened, about 3 to 4 minutes. Remove from heat and stir in salt, pepper, sour cream and Parmesan cheese, and set aside.

Meanwhile, bring a large pot of water to a boil and cook pasta per package directions until done. Drain well.

In a very large bowl mix together the pasta and sauce, then fold in the grated cheeses until well combined. Place mixture into a lightly buttered, 9-by-13-inch baking pan.

Sprinkle with Herb Bread Crumbs and bake in a 375° F oven for about 30 minutes, or until pasta is heated through, sides are slightly bubbling and top is golden brown.

Bolognese Meat Sauce with Chianti for Pasta

Makes 12 cups of sauce—great for freezing!

2 Tbsp. olive oil
1 lb. pork butt,
   cut in 1-inch chunks
1 lb. beef chuck,
   cut in 1-inch chunks
1 cup small-diced onion
3/4 cup small-diced celery
1/2 cup chopped mushrooms
3/4 cup small-diced carrot
1/2 cup small-diced
   green pepper
2 Tbsp. minced garlic
1/4 tsp. crushed red chile flakes

1/4 tsp. dry, whole-leaf
   rosemary, crushed
1 tsp. dry, whole-leaf oregano
1 tsp. dry, leaf basil
1/2 tsp. dry, whole-leaf thyme
1 1/2 cups Chianti red wine
2 cups beef broth
2 cans (6 oz. each)
   tomato paste
2 cans (1 lb. 12 oz. each)
   pear tomatoes in juice
3/4 cup whole milk
Salt as needed

In a large heavy-bottomed Dutch oven or soup pot heat the olive oil over medium-high heat. Add the meat chunks and cook, browning on all sides, about 5 minutes. Remove from pot to a plate and set aside.

Add the onion to pot and cook, stirring often, for 1 minute. Then add the celery, mushrooms, carrot and green pepper; cook, stirring often, for 1 minute. Add the garlic and chile flakes, and stir in for 30 seconds. Add the dry herbs and wine, bring to a boil and let reduce for 2 minutes.

Add the reserved browned meat, beef broth and tomato paste. Pour in the juice from the canned tomatoes, and with clean hands add the pear tomatoes to the pot while "hand-squishing" them. Bring to a slow boil, then reduce the heat to medium-low to low to keep at a consistent, slow simmer. Cook, stirring often, for about 2 hours, until meat is very, very tender and falling apart and sauce is very thick.

Stir in milk, then remove sauce from heat and stir up sauce well, breaking apart meat and incorporating into sauce. Taste the sauce for salt, and season as needed.

Recommended serving: Serve sauce over cooked pasta with an accompanying green salad and delicious garlic bread! Extra sauce can be frozen for up to 3 months.

comfort

sides

4

Egg and Shrimp Jasmine Fried Rice

Makes 8 cups; serves 6 to 10

Rice
Makes 6 cups cooked rice
2 cups jasmine rice
1 tsp. salt
3 cups water
1 fresh or frozen kaffir lime leaf
(optional)

Fried Rice Goodies
3 eggs
1/4 tsp. salt
1 Tbsp. water
3 Tbsp. vegetable oil
1 cup (about 8 oz.) uncooked medium
shrimp, peeled, deveined, and cut/split
in half lengthwise or coarsely chopped

2 tsp. minced ginger
1/4 cup small-diced
(1/4-inch) carrot
1 Tbsp. minced garlic
2 Tbsp. minced fresh
lemongrass (optional)
1/2 cup fresh shelled peas
or thinly sliced pea pods
1/4 cup thinly sliced green onions
2 Tbsp. soy sauce

Serve with:
Additional soy sauce
Sambal oelek or Asian chili condiment
Lime wedges
Cilantro sprigs

To achieve that great "fried rice" consistency, make the rice the day before. Cook, refrigerate and then let sit at room temperature for 30 minutes before frying. Cook the rice the day before, or at least 2 hours in advance, and chill.

To cook in a rice cooker: Rinse the rice in a strainer until the water runs clear. DRAIN WELL, then place in the rice cooker with all the remaining rice ingredients. Stir well, cover and steam until tender, per manufacturer's directions. After rice is cooked, fluff with a fork, let cool, then refrigerate.

To cook without a rice cooker: Preheat oven to 400° F. Rinse the rice in a strainer until the water runs clear. Shake rice and DRAIN WELL. Place rice in a large saucepan with remaining rice ingredients. Place pan over high heat, bring to a boil and stir. Quickly cover pan with a piece of foil AND a tight-fitting lid. Place in preheated oven and cook for 15 to 20 minutes, or until tender. After rice is cooked, immediately remove the lid and foil. Fluff rice with a fork, let cool, then refrigerate.

When ready to finish the dish, have all remaining ingredients prepared and within reach of the range. Cook the eggs and let them cool while you fry the rice.

To cook the eggs: In a small bowl, whisk eggs with the salt and water. Heat 1 Tbsp. of the oil in a wok or heavy, large, nonstick skillet until hot. Add the eggs and, with a spatula, lift eggs as they cook, letting uncooked part run underneath until set. Transfer eggs to a cutting board. Let cool, then cut eggs into 1/4-inch strips.

To fry the rice: Heat the remaining 2 Tbsp. oil in the same wok over medium-high heat. Add shrimp and stir-fry until just turning pink, about 15 seconds. Add the ginger, carrot, garlic, lemongrass and cooked rice. Stir-fry 2 minutes. Add the peas, green onions and shredded eggs. Stir-fry for 1 minute, until heated through, then drizzle with soy sauce and toss well.

Serve immediately and pass the soy, chili condiment, lime and cilantro separately for guests to "customize" and season their rice the way they like it.

Steamed Asparagus with Easy Citrus Chive Hollandaise
Serves 4 to 6; makes about 1 1/2 to 2 cups of hollandaise

2 bunches of fat asparagus (about 2 lb.)

Hollandaise
1 Tbsp. orange juice concentrate
2 tsp. fresh lemon juice
1 Tbsp. cream cheese
1 Tbsp. finely minced shallot

2 egg yolks
1 cup (2 sticks) melted butter
   (I used salted butter)
1/4 tsp. Tabasco Sauce
1 Tbsp. minced fresh chives
1 Tbsp. orange zest, finely chopped
Garnish: fresh chives, thinly sliced

Wash asparagus and with a paring knife trim the bottom 3 inches (the woody tough part) off and discard. Set aside.

To make the hollandaise: Combine orange juice, lemon juice, cream cheese and shallot; place over a double boiler. Whisk until smooth. Add the egg yolks and whisk for about 30 seconds, until the mixture is frothy and warm to the touch, being careful not to get eggs too hot. Slowly begin whisking in the butter in a small strand about as big as a strand of spaghetti. When all the butter has been added, the mixture will become smooth and thick. Fold in chives and orange zest.

To serve: Bring 2 inches of water to a boil in a large pan. Set asparagus in a steaming rack, place over boiling water and cover. Steam for about 1 minute or until just tender but not overcooked. Serve hot, sprinkled with a little salt if desired and dolloped with hollandaise.

sides

Wild Mushroom Mashed Potatoes

Makes about 6 1-cup servings

2 1/2 lb. russet potatoes,
   peeled and cut in halves or
   thirds, depending on size
   (about 3 jumbo potatoes)
Pinch of salt
1/2 cup milk or half-and-half
1/4 tsp. white pepper
6 Tbsp. butter
1 tsp. salt (more or less to taste)

2 tsp. butter or margarine
1 Tbsp. finely minced
   fresh garlic
2 cups finely chopped
   assorted mushrooms*
2 Tbsp. dry sherry (optional)

Garnish: minced fresh chives
   or parsley (optional)

Place potatoes in a very large pot and cover with water at least 3 inches above potatoes. Add a pinch of salt. Bring to a boil then reduce heat and cook on a low boil until completely fork tender, about 20 to 30 minutes.

Meanwhile, in a small pan over low heat combine the milk, white pepper, 6 Tbsp. butter and the 1 tsp. salt. Heat until the butter is melted and the milk is warm. Do not boil. Keep warm.

In a large nonstick skillet, heat the 2 tsp. butter over medium-high heat. Add garlic and mushrooms, and sauté for about 3 minutes—until thoroughly cooked and all moisture has evaporated. Add sherry and sauté 1 to 1 1/2 minutes more. Remove from heat.

When potatoes are cooked, drain them well in a large colander, then return them to the pot. Shake pot over low heat about 30 seconds to dry out any remaining water. Remove from the heat and add half the hot liquid mixture. (Both the potatoes and the liquid must be hot.) With a heavy-duty whisk or masher, mash the potatoes. Then add remaining liquid and whip/mash up the potatoes until they are fluffy. Mix in the mushrooms and mound potatoes in a large warm bowl. Sprinkle with minced chives or parsley.

* Chef's Note: Wild mushrooms, such as morels, chanterelles and fresh porcini, are preferable. Or use domestic mushrooms such as button and shiitake or a mixture of domestic and wild mushrooms. If fresh wild mushrooms are not available, substitute rehydrated dried ones such as morels and porcini. To rehydrate, pour boiling water over to just cover and let steep until softened. Drain before using.

mains

5

Grilled Salmon with Mushroom Vinaigrette
Serves 4; makes 1 cup of vinaigrette

Mushroom Vinaigrette
2 Tbsp. olive oil
1 cup sliced crimini mushrooms
1 cup sliced and stemmed
　shiitake mushrooms
Pinch crushed red chile flakes
1 Tbsp. minced shallots
2 tsp. minced fresh ginger
2 tsp. minced fresh garlic
1 Tbsp. soy sauce

3 Tbsp. seasoned rice wine vinegar
3 Tbsp. olive oil
1 tsp. finely zested lemon peel

4 salmon fillet portions, skinless
　(about 1 3/4 lb.)
1 to 2 Tbsp. olive oil
Kosher salt and pepper
Lemon wheels and fresh chives
　for garnish, if desired

To make the Mushroom Vinaigrette: In a large sauté pan heat the 2 Tbsp. of olive oil over medium-high heat and then add the mushrooms. Sauté the mushrooms, stirring often, until tender—about 2 minutes. Increase heat to high and add the chile flakes, shallots, ginger and garlic. Sauté for another minute, stirring often. Do not brown garlic.

Quickly add the soy sauce and vinegar, bring to a boil and cook 30 seconds, then remove from the heat. Transfer to a bowl and let cool while you grill the salmon. When cooled, stir in the 3 Tbsp. of olive oil and the lemon zest.

To grill salmon and serve: Heat your grill to hot. Meanwhile, place 1 or 2 Tbsp. of olive oil on a large dinner plate, swipe the salmon fillets through it on each side and then season them well with salt and pepper. Place on hot grill and cook, creating nice crisscross marks on each side of the salmon. Cook fish to an internal temperature of 120° – 125° F for a nice opaque center. Different-size salmon fillets will cook differently; just use good judgment and try to not overcook your salmon.

Serve immediately, topped with some of the Mushroom Vinaigrette and garnished with lemon wheels and thinly sliced chives.

Sake Teriyaki Flank Steak

Serves 4 to 6

1 1/2 lb. flank steak

Marinade
3/4 cup soy sauce
1/4 cup sake
1 Tbsp. minced fresh ginger
1 Tbsp. minced garlic
3/4 cup sugar

1/2 tsp. crushed red chile flakes
2 Tbsp. sesame oil
1/4 cup thinly sliced green onions
2 Tbsp. toasted sesame seeds

Garnish: very thin extreme-bias-cut
green onions

Trim steak of any outer pieces of fat or silver skin.

In a blender or food processor, combine all the marinade ingredients
except the green onions and sesame seeds, and process until well
combined. Pour marinade into a glass bowl or large zipper-lock bag. Add
the green onions and sesame seeds. Place steak into marinade, move
it around to coat all surfaces (make sure beef is entirely covered) and
seal or cover. Refrigerate a minimum of 4 hours or as long as 1 day.

When marinating is complete, remove steak from marinade and drain
it well (Note: If you would like to use the marinade for drizzling on the meat
after cooking, you must bring it to a boil for 2 minutes before using,
as there was raw beef in it. I like to slow-simmer it for about 8 minutes
or until reduced to 1 cup for a thicker drizzle!)

You can either grill or sauté the flank steak. If grilling, a medium-hot,
high fire is best. Grill meat 3 to 4 minutes per side, for rare. (Or sear in
a sauté pan, 3 to 4 minutes per side, in 2 Tbsp. vegetable oil over
medium-high heat.) This marinade has sugar in it, so you need to be careful
that you don't burn or blacken the outside of the meat too much, too
quickly. Let it sit about 5 minutes before serving, allowing juices to settle.

To serve: Slice thinly, at an angle, across the grain. Serve sprinkled
with green onions.

mains

Seared Scallops with Lemon Herb & Olive Vinaigrette

Serves 4; makes 3/4 cup vinaigrette

1 1/2 lb. very large
  sea scallops
Salt and pepper to taste

Vinaigrette
6 Tbsp. extra virgin olive oil
2 Tbsp. fresh lemon juice
2 tsp. minced fresh
  lemon zest
1 Tbsp. very finely minced
  fresh lemon verbena
  (or other herbs such as
  basil or lemon thyme)

1 Tbsp. very thinly
  sliced chives
1 Tbsp. fresh chive flowers
  (optional)
1 Tbsp. minced fresh parsley
2 Tbsp. very, very finely
  diced red bell pepper
2 Tbsp. very finely diced
  kalamata olives
1/8 tsp. crushed red
  chile flakes
1/2 tsp. minced fresh garlic
1/4 tsp. salt

To make the vinaigrette: Mix all ingredients together well and refrigerate until needed. Bring to room temperature before serving.

To finish the recipe: Heat a large nonstick sauté pan or skillet over high heat until hot. Pat scallops very dry with a paper towel. Sprinkle scallops lightly on each side with salt and pepper to taste.

Cook scallops in two batches so as not to crowd pan. Sear on the first side, cooking only until the scallops are golden and have a nice crust, about 1 1/2 to 2 minutes. Turn the scallops over and repeat. Do not overcook scallops; they are best cooked quick and hot.

Remove to a plate and quickly cook the remaining scallops.

To serve: Divide the scallops among 4 plates and spoon on about 3 heaping Tbsp. of the vinaigrette (be sure to stir well before using) per plate.

Chef's Note: This vinaigrette is also really nice on halibut or sea bass.

Star Anise Sprinkle for Chicken or Duck
Makes 1/2 cup

Apply spice blends more liberally than just salt and pepper
since there are a lot of other ingredients besides the S&P.
Also, you may want to put the spices on a little while before
cooking to allow the flavors time to penetrate. Use about
1/2 tsp. per small chicken or duck breast or about 1 Tbsp.
for a whole bird.

This sprinkle is also delicious on fresh tuna, sautéd carrots,
grilled onions or steamed jasmine rice.

2 whole cinnamon sticks, broken into pieces
1/4 cup star anise
2 tsp. whole black peppercorns
1 tsp. whole coriander seeds
1 1/2 tsp. dry orange peel
1/4 cup kosher salt
2 Tbsp. sugar

In a spice grinder or clean, small coffee grinder, process
spices to a medium-ground consistency; do not grind too
fine. Mix spices with salt and sugar.

mains

"New Century" Chicken Veronique with Green & Red Grapes

Serves 4

2 Tbsp. flour
1 tsp. salt
1/8 tsp. black pepper
4 boneless, skinless
   chicken breast halves
2 Tbsp. butter
2 Tbsp. olive oil
2 Tbsp. finely minced shallot
1 1/2 cups mixed seedless

red and green grapes
3 Tbsp. finely chopped
   fresh tarragon
1 1/2 tsp. minced
   fresh thyme
3/4 cup high-quality, dry white wine
3/4 cup heavy whipping cream
4 fresh tarragon sprigs

In a small bowl mix together the flour, salt and pepper. Lay chicken breasts out on a piece of plastic wrap and sprinkle them with the seasoned flour on each side. (If breasts are really thick, first pound out between two pieces of plastic wrap to slightly flatten.)

Meanwhile, heat a large nonstick skillet over medium-high heat until hot. Add the butter and oil; when hot, add the chicken breasts.

Sauté until golden brown on each side, about 4 to 5 minutes per side, and cooked through. Remove from pan and keep chicken warm. (Do not wash pan.)

Immediately place chicken-cooking pan back on burner, add shallots and sauté for about 30 seconds, being careful not to brown. Then add the grapes, chopped tarragon, thyme and wine. Increase heat to high and cook for about 1 more minute until wine has slightly evaporated. Add the cream, bring to a boil and cook at a slow boil for about 5 to 6 minutes, or until reduced and sauce-like—it should coat a spoon nicely. Taste sauce and adjust seasoning with more salt if desired.

To serve, place a chicken breast on each dinner plate and divide sauce evenly. Garnish with tarragon sprigs.

Wild Turkey Pork Chops with Cider Glazed Apples & Onions

Serves 4

4 thick-cut (1- to 1 1/2-inch)
   pork chops such as loin chops
2 Tbsp. olive oil, divided
1/2 tsp. salt
1 medium Granny Smith apple,
   with skin, cored and thinly sliced
3/4 cup thinly sliced red onion
3 Tbsp. Wild Turkey whiskey
Garnish: fresh sage leaves
   (optional)

Wild Turkey Marinade
1 Tbsp. brown sugar
1/2 cup apple cider
1 1/2 tsp. Dijon mustard
2 Tbsp. Wild Turkey whiskey
1 tsp. grated lemon rind
1/8 tsp. crushed red chile flakes
2 Tbsp. cider vinegar
1/4 tsp. dry rubbed sage

Mix all marinade ingredients together and place in a large zipper-lock bag with pork chops. Seal bag, then shake around to distribute marinade. Refrigerate for at least 30 minutes or up to 4 hours.

Preheat oven to 375° F. After marinating, remove pork chops from marinade and RESERVE marinade in a bowl.

Heat 1 Tbsp. of the olive oil in a large nonstick pan over high heat. Season pork chops on each side with salt, place in pan and brown well on each side, about 3 to 4 minutes per side. Then place pan of pork chops in preheated oven and continue cooking for about 14 to 17 minutes, depending upon the cut of chops. You will want to start checking chops after about 12 minutes and cook until just done throughout.

When chops are done, remove them to a platter and keep warm. Meanwhile, pour any juices from the chop pan into the reserved marinade. Place the pan back on the stove and heat the remaining 1 Tbsp. of olive oil over medium-high heat. Add apple and onion, and cook, stirring often, until slightly browned and tender. Add the Wild Turkey and the marinade-pan juice mixture, then increase heat to high. Cook down until almost all the liquid is reduced. Remove from heat and adjust seasoning with additional salt and pepper if needed, then serve spooned over chops. Garnish with fresh sage leaves if desired.

mains

conclusions

6

Fresh Mint Ice Cream
Makes about 4 1/2 cups

4 cups heavy cream
3/4 cup sugar
1 1/2 cups packed fresh mint leaves
6 egg yolks
2 tablespoons finely chopped fresh mint

Place cream and sugar in a large heavy saucepan.
Rinse mint leaves, then tear them into cream mixture
(to bruise them). Bring mixture to a slow simmer over
medium heat.

In a bowl whisk egg yolks, then gradually whisk
in about 1 cup of the hot cream mixture.

Whisk tempered egg mixture into cream. Let just
barely simmer for about 30 seconds while whisking
continuously. Remove from heat, and continue
whisking often. Let cool to room temperature,
then chill at least 2 hours.

Strain mixture and discard mint leaves. Stir chopped
mint into cream mixture, then pour into ice cream
maker. Freeze according to manufacturers' directions.

Serve topped with shaved chocolate or hot fudge
sauce if desired.

S'mores Cocoa
Makes 1 drink

Chocolate sauce in a squeeze bottle
Graham cracker crumbs
2 Tbsp. high-quality dark chocolate sauce
3/4 cup steamed or hot milk
Marshmallow creme

Rim a coffee glass or mug with chocolate sauce,
then press rim into graham cracker crumbs.

Place dark chocolate sauce in mug; carefully stir in hot milk.
Top with a large dollop of marshmallow creme and drizzle
with chocolate sauce.

Ultimate Adult Hot Chocolate
Makes 2 1/2 cups, or 6 to 8 small servings

Hot Chocolate
2 cups heavy cream
4 ounces (about 1 cup) bittersweet
   chocolate, chopped fine or grated
Tiny pinch of salt

For Serving
Espresso or strong coffee
Hot water
Godiva Liqueur
Granulated sugar
Whipped cream
Dark and white chocolate shavings

In a heavy-bottomed saucepan heat the cream to barely a simmer, then
whisk in the chocolate. Mixture should be smooth and creamy. Serve
while still hot in heated, small demitasse or fancy teacups. (To heat cups,
fill with simmering water for a minute or so, then pour out right before
filling cups with hot chocolate.) Serve the garnishes on a fancy platter.
Guests can "thin down" chocolate with a little hot water or espresso if
desired or add liqueur or sugar (for the super-sweet-tooth) or top with
whipped cream and/or chocolate shavings.

conclusions

Lemon & Thyme Shortbread Cookies
Makes 12 cookies

A wonderful not-too-sweet cookie with big flavor.
Try making with rosemary for a different variation.

1 stick butter, softened
1 Tbsp. finely minced lemon zest
1/3 cup confectioners' sugar
1 1/4 cups all-purpose flour
1 Tbsp. chopped fresh thyme leaves
1 Tbsp. honey

In a mixing bowl with an electric mixer, beat the butter, lemon zest and sugar until light and fluffy. Add the flour and thyme, and mix until just combined. Add the honey and then mix until dough just comes together.

With lightly floured hands roll dough into a 2-inch round cylinder and wrap tightly in plastic wrap. Refrigerate until well chilled.

When ready to bake, preheat oven to 375° F. Slice dough into 12 even slices with a sharp knife and place on a baking pan.

Bake shortbread in middle of oven approximately 10 minutes or until bottom of cookies are pale golden. Remove from oven and place cookies on a cooling rack.

conclusions

Rustic Berry Tarts

Makes 4 tarts

Be sure to read recipe through before starting.

Crust
1 1/2 cups flour
1 Tbsp. poppy seeds (optional)
1 tsp. sugar
1/2 tsp. salt
6 Tbsp. cold butter, cut into small chunks
1 large egg, beaten
2 tsp. cider vinegar
2 1/2 Tbsp. ice water

Fruit Filling
2 cups quartered strawberries
  and 1 cup thinly sliced
  rhubarb OR 3 cups total
  of any fresh berries
6 Tbsp. sugar
2 tsp. flour

To make the crust: Mix the flour, poppy seeds, sugar and salt in a large bowl. Add butter and, with a pastry blender, combine until mixture forms pea-size particles. In a small separate bowl mix together **1 Tbsp.** of the beaten egg **(reserve the rest for egg wash)**, vinegar and ice water. Stir into the dry mixture with a fork, mixing until liquid is just incorporated. (If dough is too dry, add more water, 1 to 2 tsp. at a time.) Form dough into a log and wrap in plastic wrap. Chill in refrigerator for 10 to 20 minutes.

To make Fruit Filling: Right before assembling the tarts, place fruit in a large bowl. Sprinkle in sugar and flour. Set aside and toss together after you have rolled out the dough.

To assemble and bake tarts: Preheat oven to 400° F. Cut dough into 4 equal portions. Working with 1 piece of dough at a time, press the portion into a flat round disk. On a lightly floured surface roll out dough into a 1/8-inch-thick, 6- to 6-1/2-inch circle, pressing in sides as needed to keep it round. Cover with plastic while you roll out the remaining pieces.

Divide filling evenly among the rolled tart shells, heaping it in the center of each. Gather up the crust edges around the filling, bringing about 1 1/2 inches of the dough over the fruit and pinching it as needed to make an open-face tart. Be careful not to get any holes in crust. If this happens, pinch shut.

With a spatula, carefully remove each tart to a lightly pan-sprayed or parchment-papered baking sheet. Whisk 1 tsp. of water into the reserved beaten egg and lightly brush the dough of tarts. Sprinkle the tart tops lightly with sugar.

Bake for about 30 minutes or until the crust is golden brown and the filling is bubbling; cooking time will vary with different ovens.

conclusions

Favorite Java Chocolate Chip Cookies

Makes 2 1/2 dozen cookies

I like the addition of espresso to these classic cookies.

6 oz. salted butter
1 cup brown sugar
1/4 cup sugar
1 Tbsp. instant espresso powder
1 Tbsp. vanilla extract
1 egg
1 3/4 cups flour
3/4 tsp. baking soda
3/4 tsp. salt
1 cup chopped pecans, lightly toasted in a 350° F oven
1 cup semisweet chocolate chips

Preheat oven to 375° F.

In a mixing bowl with a whip attachment, cream together the butter, sugars and espresso powder until fluffy. Then add the vanilla and egg, and mix until creamy.

Meanwhile, sift together the flour, baking soda and salt, then add these dry ingredients into creamed mixture and mix until well incorporated. Stir in the pecans and the chocolate chips.

Drop cookies on an ungreased baking sheet by 2 tablespoonfuls and bake for about 8 - 10 minutes. Cool on a rack.

conclusions

"Over 21" Jack Daniel's Holiday Fruit Cake

Makes 6 mini-loaves

1 cup chopped dried pineapple
1 cup chopped dried apricots
1 1/2 cups dried tart cherries
1 cup golden raisins
1/3 cup currants
1 1/4 cups chopped dried mango
3/4 cup boiling water
1/2 pound (2 sticks) butter, SOFTENED (very important!)
1/2 cup sugar
1/2 cup brown sugar
1/4 cup molasses
1 1/2 tsp. vanilla extract
2 tsp. orange zest
2 tsp. lemon zest
6 eggs
1/4 cup Jack Daniel's whiskey
1 3/4 cups flour
1 1/2 tsp. ground allspice
1/2 tsp. ground ginger
1/2 tsp. ground cinnamon
1/2 tsp. ground nutmeg
1 cup chopped hazelnuts
1 cup chopped walnuts
1 cup chopped pecans
1 cup whole almonds

Glaze
1/4 cup water
1/2 cup brown sugar
1/2 cup Jack Daniel's whiskey

In a large bowl toss together the dried fruits, then pour the boiling water over the fruit and toss again. Cover with plastic wrap and let sit for 24 hours at room temperature, stirring occasionally.
(continued)

Preheat oven to 300° F.

In a mixing bowl whip the butter (be sure it's super-softened!) on medium-high speed with the white and brown sugars for about 4 minutes or until fluffy. Add the molasses and then the vanilla and zests. On medium speed add 1 egg at a time, beating 1 minute between each addition. Mix in Jack Daniel's. Mixture should be whipped until it is smooth and silky.

In a sifter combine flour and spices. Remove bowl from mixer and sift in dry ingredients, folding into egg mixture until well incorporated.

Separately, in a very large bowl mix together plumped fruits and nuts. Add cake batter and fold into the fruit and nuts until well coated.

Divide mixture (about 1 1/2 cups each) among 6 buttered, nonstick mini-loaf pans (6-by-3-by-2 inch) or disposable aluminum mini-loaf pans. Smooth out batter, then bang each pan on the counter to release any air bubbles.

Place pans on a baking sheet and bake for about 45 to 55 minutes, or until set and cooked through.

Meanwhile make the glaze: In a very small saucepan combine the water and brown sugar, and bring to a boil over high heat. Boil for 1 minute, remove from the heat and cool to room temperature. Then whisk in the Jack Daniel's.

When cakes come out of the oven, remove from pan and place bottom up on a cooling rack set over a baking sheet. With a pastry brush, brush the glaze liberally on the bottom and sides of cakes while still warm. Do this quite a few times. Then turn cakes top side up and brush with more of the glaze. Keep brushing with glaze on all surfaces every 20 minutes or so until all of the glaze is used up. Cover cakes with plastic wrap and let sit overnight.

To wrap cakes: Wrap each cake individually with plastic wrap, then wrap in parchment paper. Seal with Christmas stickers and ribbon or raffia and baubles. If desired, write recipe name, baker and date on outside wrapper with a fine permanent marker or metallic pen.

Store cake at room temperature until ready to give.

Chocolate Peanut Fudge Cakes
with Peanut Butter Cream
Makes 6 individual cakes

4 oz. unsweetened chocolate
12 Tbsp. (1 1/2 sticks) butter
1/4 cup creamy peanut butter
4 large eggs
1/2 cup flour
2 cups sugar
1 tsp. vanilla extract

1 cup coarsely chopped, unsalted,
  dry-roasted peanuts

Peanut Butter Cream
1/2 cup heavy cream
2 Tbsp. creamy peanut butter
2 Tbsp. powdered sugar

Preheat oven to 350° F.

Combine chocolate, butter and peanut butter in a metal bowl and
place over a pot of just-simmering water, or use a double boiler. Stir
the mixture until the chocolate and butter are just melted. Set aside.

In a mixing bowl, mix eggs, flour, sugar and vanilla until glossy, about
2 minutes. Then, mix in the melted chocolate-butter mixture until just
combined. Stir in the peanuts.

Lightly pan-spray and flour oversized (Texas-style) muffin pans.
Divide the batter into the 6 muffin cups.

Bake in the preheated oven for about 34 minutes. The cakes will be
slightly gooey in the center. Let the cakes cool in the pans for 8 minutes,
then un-pan and cool the cakes right side up on a wire rack.

To make the Peanut Butter Cream and serve: Place cream, peanut butter
and powdered sugar in a bowl and whip until just softly peaked.

Serve cakes while still warm, or totally cool them and individually wrap
in plastic wrap until needed. (The cakes keep this way for up to 4 days.)
Serve the cakes at room temperature or warm just slightly in the
microwave on high power for about 20 to 30 seconds or until just warm.
Serve the cakes topped with a dollop of the Peanut Butter Cream.

conclusions

Aïoli
Martini Aïoli, 12
Quick Basil Aïoli, 27

Anise
Star Anise Sprinkle for
Chicken or Duck, 57

Appetizers, 11–16
Flat Bread Crisps with
Smoked Salmon &
Chive Sour Cream, 16

Gin Infused Prawns with
Martini Aïoli, 12

Ribbons of Roasted
Peppers & Herb Goat
Cheese on Crostini, 15

Roasted Tiny Red Potatoes
with Caviar & Shallot Sour
Cream or Gorgonzola
Bacon & Walnuts, 11

Asparagus
Steamed Asparagus with
Easy Citrus Chive
Hollandaise, 47

Bacon
Brown Sugar & Pepper
Glazed Bacon, 35

Spinach Salad with
Apples & Warm Bacon
Vinaigrette, 24

Basil
Quick Basil Aïoli, 27

Beef
Sake Teriyaki Flank
Steak, 53

Beets
Golden Beet Salad with
Arugula & Balsamic
Vinaigrette, 23

Berries
Rustic Berry Tarts, 71

Bread
Crostini, 15

Flat Bread Crisps with
Smoked Salmon &
Chive Sour Cream, 16

Garlic Burger Buns, 39

Bread crumbs
Herb Bread Crumbs, 40

Buns
Garlic Burger Buns, 39

Cake
Chocolate Peanut Fudge
Cakes with Peanut
Butter Cream, 77

"Over 21" Jack Daniel's
Holiday Fruit Cake, 75–76

Cheese
4 Cheese "Mac" with
Herb Bread Crumbs, 40

Ribbons of Roasted
Peppers & Herb Goat
Cheese on Crostini, 15

Roasted Tiny Red
Potatoes with Gorgonzola
Bacon & Walnuts, 11

Vine Ripe Tomato & Fresh
Mozzarella "Caprese" Tower
with Quick Basil Aïoli, 27

Chicken
"New Century" Chicken
Veronique with Green &
Red Grapes, 58

Star Anise Sprinkle for
Chicken or Duck, 57

Chocolate
Chocolate Peanut Fudge
Cakes with Peanut Butter
Cream, 77.

See also Cocoa and Cookies

Cocktails
Love Potion No. 10, 8
Zoë Cocktail, 8

Cocoa
S'mores Cocoa, 67

Ultimate Adult Hot
Chocolate, 67

Cookies
Favorite Java Chocolate
Chip Cookies, 72

Lemon & Thyme
Shortbread Cookies, 68

Cornmeal Griddle Cakes, 35

Crostini, 15
Ribbons of Roasted
Peppers & Herb Goat
Cheese on Crostini, 15

Duck
Star Anise Sprinkle for
Chicken or Duck, 57

Eggs
"Denver" Breakfast Bake
for a Crowd, 32

Egg and Shrimp Jasmine
Fried Rice, 46-47

Fruit cake
"Over 21" Jack Daniel's
Holiday Fruit Cake, 75–76

Garlic Burger Buns, 39

Hamburgers
The Best Blue Cheese-
Stuffed Burgers on Garlic
Buns with Vine-Ripe Tomatoes
& Horseradish Spread, 36

Hollandaise
Easy Citrus Chive
Hollandaise, 47

Horseradish Spread, 36

Ice cream
Fresh Mint Ice Cream, 64

Lemon
Lemon Herb & Olive
Vinaigrette, 54

Lemon & Thyme
Shortbread Cookies, 68

Macaroni
4 Cheese "Mac" with Herb
Bread Crumbs, 40

Marinade
Sake Teriyaki, 53
Wild Turkey (whiskey), 61

Mint
Fresh Mint Ice Cream, 64

Mushrooms
Mushroom Vinaigrette, 52

Wild Mushroom Mashed
Potatoes, 48

Pancakes
Cornmeal Griddle Cakes, 35

Pasta
Bolognese Meat Sauce
with Chianti for Pasta, 43

4 Cheese "Mac" with Herb
Bread Crumbs, 40

Peanut Butter Cream, 77

Pork
Wild Turkey Pork Chops
with Cider Glazed Apples
& Onions, 61

Potatoes
Roasted Tiny Red Potatoes
with Caviar & Shallot Sour
Cream or Gorgonzola
Bacon & Walnuts, 11

Wild Mushroom Mashed
Potatoes, 48

Prawns
Gin Infused Prawns with
Martini Aïoli, 12.
See also Shrimp

Rice
Egg and Shrimp Jasmine
Fried Rice, 46–47

Salad, 20–27
Golden Beet Salad with
Arugula & Balsamic
Vinaigrette, 23

Merlot "Double Red Wine"
Vinaigrette with Simple
Seasonal Greens, 20

Orange, Avocado & Red
Onion "Jumble" with
Poppyseed Vinaigrette, 23

Spinach Salad with
Apples & Warm Bacon
Vinaigrette, 24

Vine Ripe Tomato & Fresh
Mozzarella "Caprese" Tower
with Quick Basil Aïoli, 27

Salmon
Flat Bread Crisps with
Smoked Salmon & Chive
Sour Cream, 16

Grilled Salmon with
Mushroom Vinaigrette, 52

Sauce
Bolognese Meat Sauce
with Chianti for Pasta, 43

Easy Citrus Chive
Hollandaise, 47

Scallops
Seared Scallops with
Lemon Herb & Olive
Vinaigrette, 54

Shortbread
Lemon & Thyme
Shortbread Cookies, 68

Shrimp
Egg and Shrimp Jasmine
Fried Rice, 46–47.
See also Prawns

Simple Syrup, 8

Soup
Ribollita Soup with Extra
Virgin Olive Oil, 28

Spinach Salad with Apples &
Warm Bacon Vinaigrette, 24

Spreads
Horseradish Spread, 36

Steak
Sake Teriyaki Flank Steak,
53

Tarts
Rustic Berry Tarts, 71

Tomato
Vine Ripe Tomato & Fresh
Mozzarella "Caprese" Tower
with Quick Basil Aïoli, 27

Vinaigrette
Balsamic Vinaigrette, 23

Lemon Herb & Olive
Vinaigrette (for scallops),
54

Merlot "Double Red Wine"
Vinaigrette, 20

Mushroom Vinaigrette
(for salmon), 52

Poppyseed Vinaigrette, 23

Warm Bacon Vinaigrette, 24

index

Dishing out sumptuous food and witty prose, **Kathy Casey** is a longtime fixture on the stages of both Northwest and national cuisine. At her one-of-a-kind facility, Kathy Casey Food Studios®, she focuses on concept and menu development for restaurants and food companies nationwide. Casey also conducts cooking classes for the public and plays host for numerous special events. Named as one of the 25 "hot new American chefs" by *Food & Wine* magazine and hailed by Craig Claiborne of *The New York Times* as an "inventor of dishes that dazzle the eye and the palate," she has a gregarious attitude that is manifested in her vibrant and delectable cuisine.

When not in the kitchen, Casey pens the monthly column "Dishing" for *The Seattle Times*. She has also authored *Pacific Northwest: The Beautiful Cookbook*, a Julia Child Cookbook Award nominee; coauthored *Best Places Seattle Cookbook*; and most recently cooked up *Dishing with Kathy Casey*. A frequent TV show guest, Casey also hosts the PBS TV show *KCTS Cooks Live*. Visit Kathy Casey's new retail shop DISH D'LISH at Seattle's Pike Place Market.